The Visual Guide to

Asperger's Syndrome in 13-16 Year Olds

by Alis Rowe

Also by Alis Rowe

One Lonely Mind
978-0-9562693-0-0

The Girl with the Curly Hair - Asperger's and Me
978-0-9562693-2-4

The 1st Comic Book
978-0-9562693-1-7

The 2nd Comic Book
978-0-95626934-8

The 3rd Comic Book
978-0-9562693-3-1

The 4th Comic Book
978-15086839-7-1

Websites:
www.alisrowe.co.uk
www.thegirlwiththecurlyhair.co.uk
www.womensweightlifting.co.uk

Social Media:
www.facebook.com/thegirlwiththecurlyhair
www.twitter.com/curlyhairedalis

The Visual Guide to

Asperger's Syndrome in 13-16 Year Olds

by Alis Rowe

Lonely Mind Books
London

For teenagers with Asperger's Syndrome and their parents and teachers

hello

This book was written for teenagers in secondary school who have Asperger's Syndrome or Autism Spectrum Disorder, their parents (to read together or separately), and teachers.

The Girl with the Curly Hair takes us on a visual journey and explains how her ASD affects her in day to day school life. She talks about her dislike of group work, her dislike of P.E. and Drama, her desire to spend time alone after school and at the weekends and, her meltdowns.

This is an important book to help teenagers feel less alone during what can be a very confusing and stressful period in their lives.

I hope you enjoy this book.

Alis aka The Girl with the Curly Hair

WHAT IS ASPERGER'S SYNDROME?

THE GIRL WITH THE CURLY HAIR
KNOWS WHAT IT IS TO HER...

THE PERSON MIGHT FIND IT VERY HARD TO MAKE FRIENDS

THEY MIGHT NOT LIKE BEING TOUCHED BY ANYONE EXCEPT THEIR MUM

THEY MIGHT BE VERY FUSSY OR PARTICULAR WITH FOOD

THEY MIGHT FIND IT REALLY HARD TO CONCENTRATE AT SCHOOL

THEY MIGHT PREFER TO PLAY/BE ON THEIR OWN RATHER THAN WITH OTHER PEOPLE

THEY MIGHT NOT FEEL ABLE TO USE PUBLIC TOILETS AND INSTEAD WAIT UNTIL THEY GET HOME

NORMAL THINGS ARE LIKELY TO BE VERY ANXIETY-PROVOKING, EVEN THINGS LIKE GOING TO THE SHOP

THEY MIGHT BE SENSITIVE TO CLOTHES AND PREFER ANY INSIDE LABELS ARE CUT OFF

THEY MIGHT FLAP THEIR ARMS

THE GIRL WITH THE CURLY HAIR SAYS THAT A PERSON WITH ASPERGER'S SYNDROME (AUTISM SPECTRUM DISORDER) IS A VERY SPECIAL SORT OF PERSON

MOST PEOPLE ARE KNOWN AS NTS

OTHER PEOPLE ARE KNOWN AS ASS...

AUTISM SPECTRUM (AS)

A PERSON ON THE AUTISM SPECTRUM

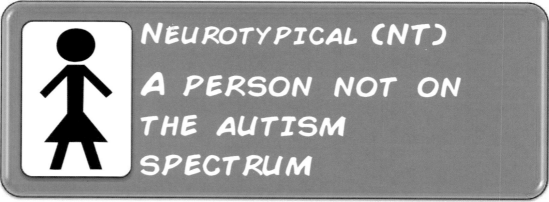

NEUROTYPICAL (NT)

A PERSON NOT ON THE AUTISM SPECTRUM

THERE ARE FEWER ASS THAN THERE ARE NTS

AN AS AND NT THINK AND SPEAK
IN DIFFERENT WAYS

AND

THEY OFTEN LIKE DOING DIFFERENT
THINGS TOO...

NT Peers	The Girl with the Curly Hair
They like eating sweets and chocolate	She only likes eating dark chocolate
They like hanging out with each other after school	She likes to be alone in her bedroom after school
They love dressing up in trendy clothes and trying on makeup	She likes wearing just a couple of outfits and has no interest in makeup
They love going to the movies or the shopping centre	She finds the movies and the shopping centre very overwhelming
They like riding their bikes in the park	She feels frustrated because, although she can ride with them, she still uses stabilisers
They HATE maths and prefer drama class	She loves maths and can do it very easily in her head
They like sleepovers	She can only ever sleep when she's at home in her own bed

IT'S IMPORTANT THAT THEY ARE
AWARE OF THEIR DIFFERENCES

AND

BE UNDERSTANDING AND PATIENT
WITH EACH OTHER SO THAT THEY
CAN BE FRIENDS!

IN HER CLASS AT SCHOOL, SHE IS THE ONLY AS...

THERE ARE 30 NTS...

SHE KNOWS SHE IS DIFFERENT AND
FEELS LEFT OUT A LOT

IT'S LIKE BEING STUCK INSIDE
A GLASS JAR LOOKING OUT AT
EVERYONE ELSE

21

THE TEENAGE YEARS ARE PARTICULARLY DIFFICULT BECAUSE THERE ARE A LOT OF NEW CHALLENGES, E.G.

A NEW SCHOOL

- MAKING NEW FRIENDS
- GETTING USED TO A VARIED TIMETABLE
- KEEPING ORGANISED WITH HOMEWORK
- JOINING CLUBS AND TEAMS

SENSORY

- CROWDED CORRIDORS
- FLICKERING OR BRIGHT LIGHTING
- BELLS RINGING
- LOTS OF STUDENTS IN GROUPS LAUGHING AND SHOUTING

PHYSICAL

- GROWING TALLER
- DEVELOPING HIPS AND BREASTS
- BECOMING 'CURVY'
- GROWING HAIR
- PERIODS

EMOTIONAL

- INCREASED ANGER
- MOOD SWINGS
- INCREASED SELF-AWARENESS
- STILL FEELING VERY YOUNG
- DIFFICULTY CONNECTING WITH PEERS; LITTLE INTEREST IN BOYS

ADOLESCENCE IS ARGUABLY THE
HARDEST TIME FOR EVERYONE

IT'S EVEN HARDER WHEN YOU DON'T
FIT IN

Comparison of ASD in Childhood and Adolescence

Child:
Parents are largely responsible for their child's routines and friendships;
Primary school is generally small and safe;
Teachers look after them

Adolescent:
They become aware they are 'on their own' socially;
Increased awareness of self;
Friendships become their own responsibility rather than their parents;
Secondary school is larger, complicated and variable;
Internal and external body changes

THE HARDEST BIT ABOUT
ADOLESCENCE IS USUALLY
SOCIALISING. OTHER ADOLECENTS
THE SAME AGE ARE MAKING FRIENDS
EASILY (USUALLY FRIENDS OF THE
SAME SEX

THE GIRL WITH THE CURLY HAIR

MAY WANT TO MAKE FRIENDS BUT DOESN'T KNOW HOW TO. IT DOESN'T COME NATURALLY TO HER AND SHE FEELS LIKE THERE'S A BIG GAP BETWEEN THEM...

GIRLS BECOME MORE SEGREGATED THAN BOYS IN TEENAGE YEARS

THE GIRL WITH THE CURLY HAIR WAS HYPERAWARE OF HER OWN DIFFERENCES AND DESPERATELY TRIED TO FIT IN

BUT THIS MADE HER FEEL LIKE SHE WASN'T TRUE TO HERSELF

IN TRUTH, NEUROTYPICAL GIRL INTERESTS DID NOT INTEREST HER AT ALL... OR THEY INTERESTED HER IN DIFFERENT WAYS

FOR EXAMPLE, MORE OBSESSIVELY OR MORE INTENSELY

SHE ENDS UP SPENDING MORE TIME AROUND HER MALE PEERS THAN HER FEMALE ONES

THEY SEEM TO HAVE A FEW MORE THINGS IN COMMON...

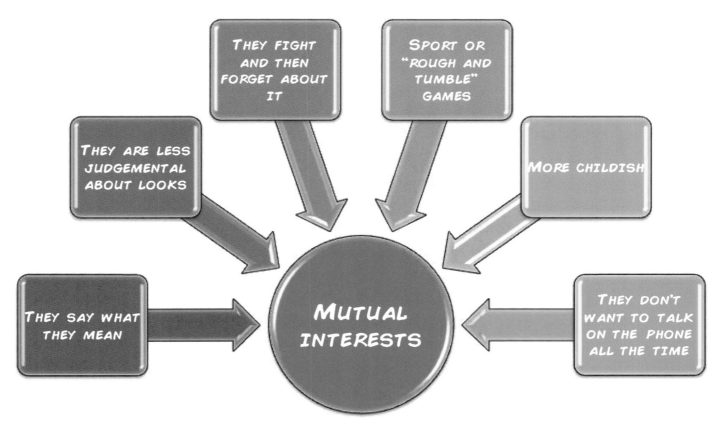

THEY FIGHT AND THEN FORGET ABOUT IT

SPORT OR "ROUGH AND TUMBLE" GAMES

THEY ARE LESS JUDGEMENTAL ABOUT LOOKS

MORE CHILDISH

THEY SAY WHAT THEY MEAN

MUTUAL INTERESTS

THEY DON'T WANT TO TALK ON THE PHONE ALL THE TIME

THIS IS **OK** – SO LONG AS SHE KNOWS THAT, DURING PUBERTY, BOYS CHANGE TOO

GIRLS WITH ASD ARE MORE IMMATURE THAN THEIR PEERS AND MAY BE VERY NAIVE WHEN IT COMES TO SEXUALITY AND PUBERTY

THE WAY BOYS CHANGE WILL AFFECT THE RELATIONSHIP SHE HAS WITH THEM

HOW DO BOYS CHANGE DURING PUBERTY?

THEY GET MORE AGGRESSIVE

THEY MIGHT OBSESS OVER GIRLS AND SEX

THEY CARE MORE ABOUT THEIR APPEARANCE

THEY ARE INTERESTED IN DATING

At school, her least favourite subjects are the ones that involve group work, such as, English, P.E., Languages, Drama...

WHAT ARE SOME OF THE REASONS THE GIRL WITH THE CURLY HAIR DISLIKES P.E.?

EVERYONE ELSE SEEMS TO HAVE JUST ONE BAG. SHE TAKES TWO EXTRA BAGS, ONE FOR TRAINERS AND ONE FOR P.E. CLOTHES

SHE FEELS LOST BECAUSE SHE NEVER KNOWS WHAT'S COMING NEXT. THERE'S NO WHITEBOARD AND NO BOOKS. THE TEACHER PREFERS TO TALK

THE SPORTS HALL IS TOO BIG AND TOO LOUD. EVERYTHING ECHOES. SHE FEELS VERY OUT OF CONTROL OF HER ENVIRONMENT AND PREFERS TO STAND AT THE EDGE OF THE HALL

SHE'S TOO ANXIOUS TO LEAVE HER BAGS IN THE LOCKER, BECAUSE THE LOCKER ROOM IS ALWAYS TOO CROWDED AND NOISY

SHE DOESN'T KNOW HOW TO USE A TENNIS RACKET. SHE DOESN'T KNOW WHAT SHE'S SUPPOSED TO BE DOING WHEN TOLD TO "PLAY TENNIS"

WHEN SHE RUNS, SOMETIMES THE OTHER CHILDREN DELIBERATELY RUN RIGHT BEHIND HER, WHICH MAKES HER FEEL ANXIOUS

SHE DOESN'T UNDERSTAND WHY P.E. IS A "LESSON" BECAUSE SHE NEVER SEEMS TO LEARN ANYTHING. MOST OF THE TIME IT SEEMS TO BE JUST RUNNING AROUND A FIELD

SHE'S ALWAYS PICKED LAST WHENEVER TEAMS ARE ORGANISED

SHE FEELS RUSHED DURING 'CHANGING' TIME. THERE'S NEVER ENOUGH TIME FOR HER TO DRESS OR UNDRESS PROPERLY

WHAT ARE SOME OF THE REASONS *THE GIRL WITH THE CURLY HAIR* DISLIKES DRAMA?

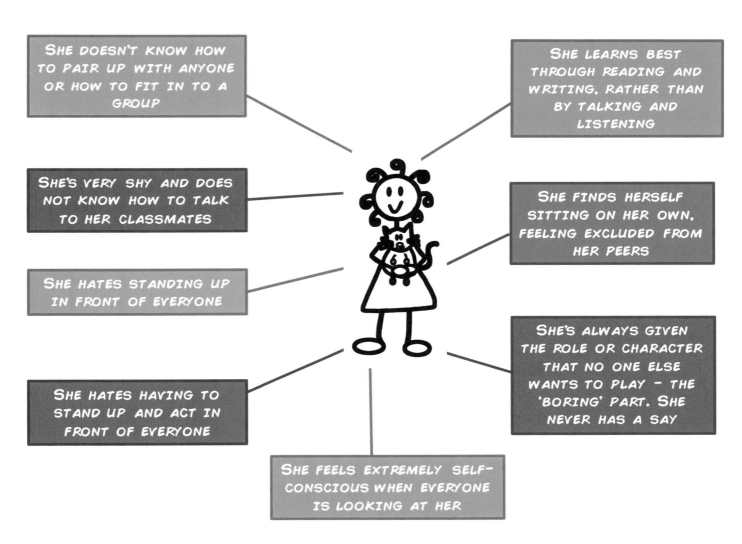

SHE DOESN'T KNOW HOW TO PAIR UP WITH ANYONE OR HOW TO FIT IN TO A GROUP

SHE LEARNS BEST THROUGH READING AND WRITING, RATHER THAN BY TALKING AND LISTENING

SHE'S VERY SHY AND DOES NOT KNOW HOW TO TALK TO HER CLASSMATES

SHE FINDS HERSELF SITTING ON HER OWN, FEELING EXCLUDED FROM HER PEERS

SHE HATES STANDING UP IN FRONT OF EVERYONE

SHE HATES HAVING TO STAND UP AND ACT IN FRONT OF EVERYONE

SHE'S ALWAYS GIVEN THE ROLE OR CHARACTER THAT NO ONE ELSE WANTS TO PLAY – THE 'BORING' PART. SHE NEVER HAS A SAY

SHE FEELS EXTREMELY SELF-CONSCIOUS WHEN EVERYONE IS LOOKING AT HER

THE SCHOOL ENVIRONMENT IS ALREADY INCREDIBLY STRESSFUL:

EVERYBODY LAUGHS AND SHOUTS A LOT AND THE SOUNDS ARE TOO LOUD AND HURT HER EARS

THE OLDER CHILDREN FRIGHTEN HER. SOMETIMES THEY SAY MEAN THINGS

THE TEACHERS TELL HER SHE NEEDS TO "SPEAK UP" WHICH MAKES HER FEEL ANXIOUS AND SHY

SHE IS EASILY SQUASHED INSIDE THE CORRIDORS WHICH MAKES HER FEEL HORRIBLE BECAUSE SHE HATES BEING TOUCHED

BREAK TIMES FEEL POINTLESS. SHE'D RATHER HAVE NO BREAKS AND GET HOME EARLIER

HER PEERS SWEAR A LOT BECAUSE THEY THINK IT'S "COOL" BUT SHE KNOWS THAT SWEARING IS BAD

SHE'S MADE FUN OF BECAUSE SHE STILL CAN'T TIE HER SHOE LACES

SHE HAS NOWHERE TO GO TO EAT LUNCH BECAUSE THE CANTEEN IS SO CROWDED AND NOISY, SO SHE DOESN'T EAT AT ALL

TEACHERS OFTEN MAKE REMARKS
THAT SHE SHOULD "INTERACT MORE"

BUT SHE PREFERS BEING ON HER
OWN

SHE IS NATURALLY QUIET UNLESS
SHE HAS SOMETHING TO SAY

Socialising is very, very hard

She only likes a small variety of foods. It's hard when everyone else is eating fresh fruit. She prefers tinned vegetables

She gets socially exhausted very quickly and can't spend long periods of time around people

Her ears are so sensitive that parties, shops and restaurants are just unbearably loud

Sometimes she laughs or smiles at the wrong time

It's hard to talk to other girls her own age. They like boys, makeup and clothes. She likes weightlifting

She doesn't have that 'street' knowledge of sex and dating behaviours, which makes her feel left out of conversations

She doesn't look in people's eyes or her body language might convey a lack of interest. They think she's being rude

Simply put, she exists 'in her own world'

She finds it stressful if she's late for bath time and bed time

Sometimes she is invited to parties but...

GOING OUT TO SOCIALISE JUST MAKES HER FEEL WORSE. IT USUALLY ONLY EVER ENDS UP ONE OF TWO WAYS:

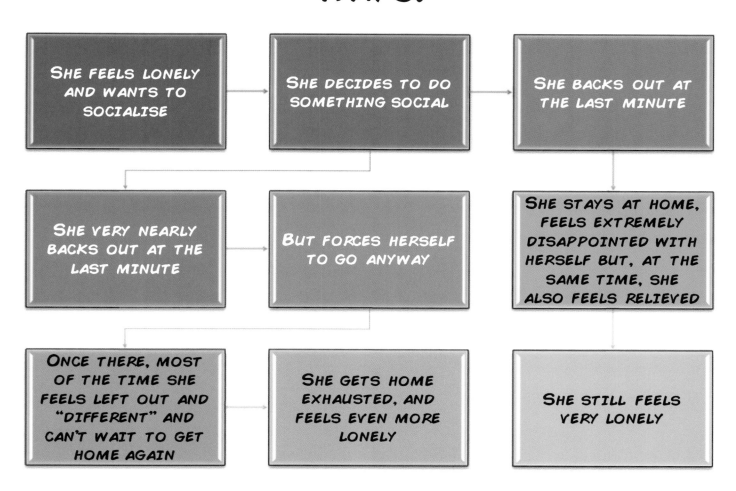

SHE FEELS LONELY AND WANTS TO SOCIALISE → SHE DECIDES TO DO SOMETHING SOCIAL → SHE BACKS OUT AT THE LAST MINUTE

SHE VERY NEARLY BACKS OUT AT THE LAST MINUTE → BUT FORCES HERSELF TO GO ANYWAY

SHE STAYS AT HOME, FEELS EXTREMELY DISAPPOINTED WITH HERSELF BUT, AT THE SAME TIME, SHE ALSO FEELS RELIEVED

ONCE THERE, MOST OF THE TIME SHE FEELS LEFT OUT AND "DIFFERENT" AND CAN'T WAIT TO GET HOME AGAIN → SHE GETS HOME EXHAUSTED, AND FEELS EVEN MORE LONELY

SHE STILL FEELS VERY LONELY

Certain sensations are too strong...

THE GIRL WITH THE CURLY HAIR
CAN BE LIKENED TO THE PRINCESS...
THEY CAN BOTH FEEL THE PEA!

THE SOUNDS OF BALLOONS POPPING CAN FEEL LIKE **EXPLOSIONS** IN HER EARS...

THE SMELL OF POPCORN CAN MAKE HER FEEL LIKE SHE'S SUFFOCATING!

SO SOMETIMES IT IS JUST EASIER FOR HER TO STAY AT HOME, RATHER THAN GO OUT SOCIALISING

THERE ARE SOME PLACES THAT MAKE HER FEEL SAFE. IT JUST TOOK SOME TIME TO FIND THEM...

THIS IS HER WHOLE WORLD...

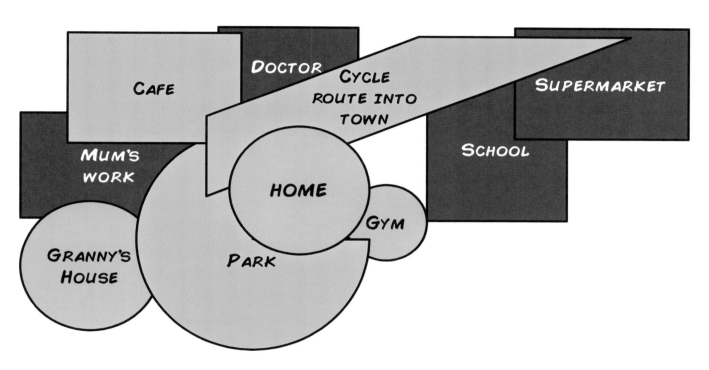

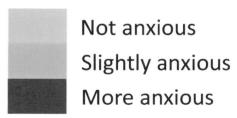

Not anxious
Slightly anxious
More anxious

SHE KNOWS THESE PLACES. SHE FEELS SAFE IN THEM. THIS IS HER "COMFORT ZONE." BEYOND THIS ZONE, SHE EXPERIENCES VERY, VERY HIGH ANXIETY

At home is her favourite place to be

She can just be a "daughter" and do those things, rather than all the other confusing roles that life requires her to be

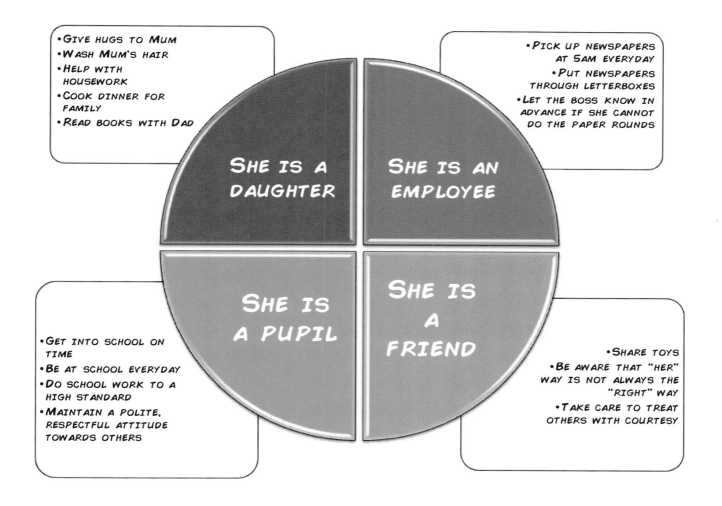

- GIVE HUGS TO MUM
- WASH MUM'S HAIR
- HELP WITH HOUSEWORK
- COOK DINNER FOR FAMILY
- READ BOOKS WITH DAD

SHE IS A DAUGHTER

- PICK UP NEWSPAPERS AT 5AM EVERYDAY
- PUT NEWSPAPERS THROUGH LETTERBOXES
- LET THE BOSS KNOW IN ADVANCE IF SHE CANNOT DO THE PAPER ROUNDS

SHE IS AN EMPLOYEE

- GET INTO SCHOOL ON TIME
- BE AT SCHOOL EVERYDAY
- DO SCHOOL WORK TO A HIGH STANDARD
- MAINTAIN A POLITE, RESPECTFUL ATTITUDE TOWARDS OTHERS

SHE IS A PUPIL

SHE IS A FRIEND

- SHARE TOYS
- BE AWARE THAT "HER" WAY IS NOT ALWAYS THE "RIGHT" WAY
- TAKE CARE TO TREAT OTHERS WITH COURTESY

By 3.20pm on school days, she's completely exhausted

MONDAY MORNING BEFORE SCHOOL SOCIAL ENERGY TANK:

MONDAY MORNING AFTER SCHOOL SOCIAL ENERGY TANK:

THIS MEANS THAT AFTER SCHOOL CLUBS ARE A "NO NO"

INSTEAD, IT'S MUCH BETTER FOR HER TO BE ALONE IN HER BEDROOM

OR ALONE, WITH HER CATS...

SHE LIKES PEOPLE BUT PREFERS ANIMALS

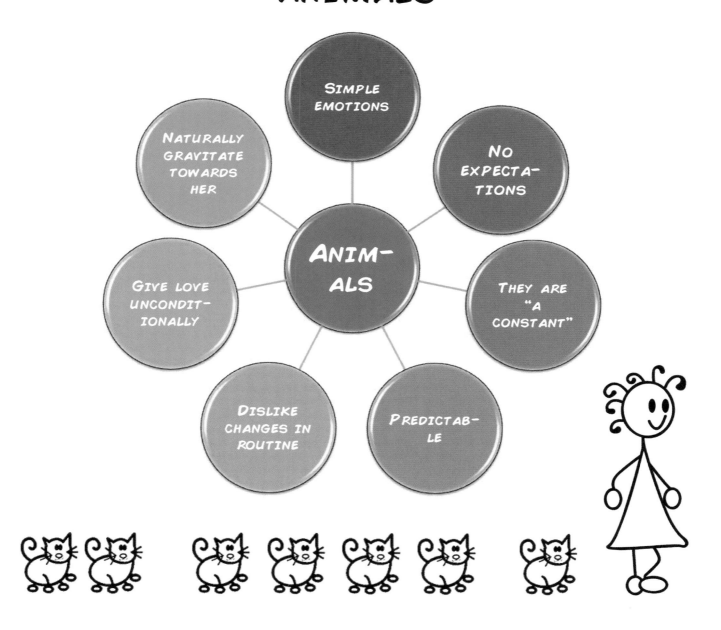

MUM AND DAD DON'T UNDERSTAND HOW SHE CAN BE SO SENSIBLE AND MATURE BUT SO IMMATURE AND NAIVE AT THE SAME TIME!

SHE EITHER ACTS LIKE A 10 YEAR OLD

OR A 50 YEAR OLD

IT SEEMS LIKE THERE ARE NO YEARS IN BETWEEN!

TANTRUMS AND MELTDOWNS HAPPEN A LOT, TYPICALLY BECAUSE OF UNPREDICTABLE THINGS SUCH AS...

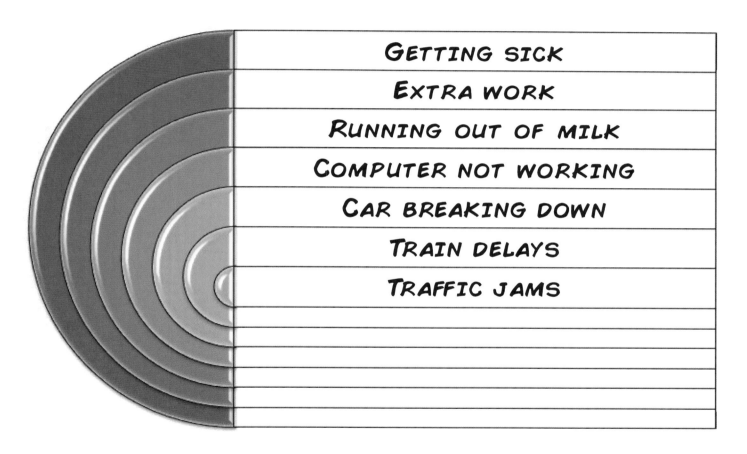

	GETTING SICK
	EXTRA WORK
	RUNNING OUT OF MILK
	COMPUTER NOT WORKING
	CAR BREAKING DOWN
	TRAIN DELAYS
	TRAFFIC JAMS

CAN YOU SEE THAT MANY OF THESE THINGS HAPPEN ON A DAILY BASIS?

MUM AND DAD WORRY ABOUT THEIR LITTLE GIRL BECAUSE SHE CAN APPEAR VERY INNOCENT AND NAIVE, E.G....

SHE CAN'T TELL WHEN SOMEONE IS MAKING A JOKE OR BEING SARCASTIC

SHE BUYS HER FRIEND A BIRTHDAY GIFT, DESPITE THE FACT HER FRIEND HAS NEVER ONCE REMEMBERED HERS

HER BELIEFS CAN EASILY BE SWAYED IF SOMEONE IS BETTER OR MORE CONFIDENT AT ASSERTING THEIR OPINION

SHE BELIEVES SHE IS PRETTY WHEN BOYS TELL HER. SHE THINKS THEY ARE BEING HONEST AND NICE

SHE CAN'T BELIEVE THAT SOMEONE WHO IS NICE TO HER FACE MIGHT BE BEING CRUEL BEHIND HER BACK

SHE BELIEVES THAT WHEN PEOPLE CRY, THEY TRULY ARE SAD AND CANNOT UNDERSTAND 'CROCODILE TEARS'

SHE GIVES CHOCOLATES AND SWEETIES TO CHILDREN SHE BABYSITS WHEN THEY TELL HER THEIR MUM ALLOWS IT

SHE WALKS HER NEIGHBOUR'S DOG REGULARLY BUT ISN'T PAID FOR IT

63

THEY KNOW THAT PLANNING IS VERY IMPORTANT

DIFFERENT SOCIAL ACTIVITIES OR EVENTS REQUIRE DIFFERENT AMOUNTS OF "PREPARATION TIME", E.G.:

EVENT	PREPARATION TIME
GOING ON HOLIDAY	ONE YEAR
GOING TO WATCH A THEATRE PERFORMANCE	AT LEAST ONE MONTH
GOING TO THE DOCTOR	AT LEAST TWO WEEKS
MEETING UP WITH A FRIEND	SEVERAL DAYS
SEEING PERSONAL TRAINER	24 HOURS
GOING TO THE SUPERMARKET	A COUPLE OF HOURS
TALKING WITH FAMILY	LESS THAN 1 HOUR

'THE DENTIST'

POSSIBLE R
DISLIKI
EXPER

LACK OF UNDERSTANDING

SENSOR

NOT UNDERSTANDING THE PURPOSE AND IMPORTANCE OF HAVING HEALTHY TEETH AND GUMS

MOUTHS ARE SENSITIVE PLACES, GENERALLY

DRILLS CAN BE VERY LOUD

INS
N
V.

(NOBODY LIKES GOING TO THE DENTIST, BUT SHE HAS VERY SENSORY-SPECIFIC REASONS TO DISLIKE IT, IN ADDITION TO STRUGGLING WITH SOCIAL CHIT CHAT AND BODY LANGUAGE, ETC.)

...NS FOR ...HE ...E

...MENTS ...BE ...OLD

MOUTH WASH MAY TASTE UNPLEASANT

INVASION OF SPACE

THE DENTIST IS PHYSICALLY VERY CLOSE

THEY TOUCH AND FEEL YOUR MOUTH

SHE NEEDS ALL QUESTIONS
ANSWERED AND ALL THINGS
EXPLAINED

NO INFORMATION MUST EVER BE
MISSING

FOR EXAMPLE, WHEN MUM AND DAD WENT TO A PARTY, IT WASN'T SUFFICIENT FOR THEM TO JUST SAY IT "WAS GOOD", I.E.

"THE PARTY... ...WAS GOOD"

SHE NEEDED A LOT MORE DETAIL:

"AT THE PARTY, WE... ...CHATTED WITH OUR FRIENDS, TOM AND JANE... ...SAW NATALIE'S DOG...

...AND THEN WE WERE BACK HOME!" ...GOT A TAXI AT 10PM... ...HAD QUICHE AND CHOCOLATE POTS FOR SUPPER...

WHEN THE GIRL WITH THE CURLY HAIR AND HER LOVED ONES TALK TO EACH OTHER, THEY HAVE LOTS OF FUN!

PEOPLE MAY
COMMUNICATE
DIFFERENTLY, BUT
THERE'S NO REASON
THEY CAN'T MEET
HALFWAY

IT JUST TAKES
SOME EFFORT AND
UNDERSTANDING
ON BOTH PARTS

NT/ASD

NT/NT

ASD/ASD

GIRLS WITH ASD ARE SPECIAL BECAUSE...

THEY HAVE A STRONG SENSE OF IDENTITY AND INDIVIDUALITY

- NON-CONFORMERS
- CREATIVE AND INNOVATIVE
- QUIRKY

THEY ARE EXCEPTIONALLY GOOD AT CERTAIN THINGS

- GIFTED
- PERFECTIONISTS
- FOCUSSED
- PASSIONATE
- DESIRE TO KNOW "WHY?"

THEY ARE HIGHLY EMOTIONAL

- CARING AND UNDERSTANDING OF OTHERS
- EMPATHETIC TOWARDS ANIMALS

THE GIRL WITH THE CURLY HAIR
KNOWS SHE WILL GET A GREAT JOB

IT'S A GOOD IDEA FOR TEENAGERS WITH ASD TO THINK ABOUT HOW THEIR SPECIAL INTERESTS COULD LEAD TO CAREERS

HERE ARE SOME SUGGESTIONS:

SPECIAL INTEREST	JOB
BUILDING THINGS OUT OF LEGO®	CONSTRUCTION, ARCHITECTURE, ENGINEERING
HOW COMPUTERS WORK	PROGRAMMING, NETWORK SYSTEMS
PLAYING SUPER MARIO BROS.® VIDEO GAMES	GRAPHIC DESIGN, PLUMBING, SOFTWARE DESIGN
REPAIRING THINGS	FACTORY MAINTENANCE, MECHANIC
HISTORY	JOURNALIST, WRITER
ANIMALS	ANIMAL TRAINER, VET, VET NURSE
SCIENCE AND SPACE	RESEARCH SCIENTIST, PHYSICIST

THE TEENAGE YEARS ARE PROBABLY
THE HARDEST YEARS OF OUR LIVES

THE GIRL WITH THE CURLY HAIR
WANTS TEENAGERS TO KNOW THEY ARE NOT ALONE

THINGS CAN - AND DO - CHANGE, FOR THE BETTER!

Many thanks for reading

Other books in The Visual Guides series at the time of writing:

The Visual Guide to Asperger's Syndrome

The Visual Guide to Asperger's Syndrome: Meltdowns and Shutdowns

The Visual Guide to Asperger's Syndrome in 5-8 Year Olds

The Visual Guide to Asperger's Syndrome in 8-11 Year Olds

The Visual Guide to Asperger's Syndrome and Anxiety

The Visual Guide to Asperger's Syndrome for the Neurotypical Partner

New titles are continually being produced so keep an eye out!

Printed in Great Britain
by Amazon